My Summer Vacation

by

Charlie Walsh

Introduction
by
Maureen Owen

60 positions for neon tetras

As Is / So & So

Berkeley 1978

"Some of these poems were printed in *Bad Breath, Barbecue Planet, Telephone, The Spirit That Moves Us* and *The Scribe*."

first edition
ISBN: 0-918842-00-x

For Gail

INTRODUCTION

Boarding the train for New York, I switch back the first page of *My Summer Vacation* by Charlie Walsh and enter a constantly shifting geography, a mysterious voyage that crosses from island to island indiscriminately while underneath a pattern is emerging, unnoticed and subliminal. A hymn quiet as a hum, that begins instantly and alters the daily overkill of information without changing it. The poet's vision that transcends the reality and at the same time reports it with utmost accuracy.

"we hymn ourselves into a passionate world."

It is the way moonlight falling across the lawn can transform the dish we are washing. The thousand facets of overkill calmed by the poet's moving center of language that goes from place to place seeing and recording everything, but not being overwhelmed by it. In these poems Charlie Walsh hurls us by ourselves on the platform and at the same time keeps us on the train hurling by. It is a feat almost magical that illuminates single gestures in rapid succession with such a penetrating light that they become instantly indelible in the mind, gestures kept forever, we can return to for clarity. He sneaks in dreams and ideas of places as easily as the actual places themselves and we find our footing slightly unsure but mingled with such adventure it never occurs to us to ask "where am I?" There is a tremendous sense that wherever the poet has taken us at a point, it's of great importance and all part of the "vacation trip."

In the Tenth Hymn he has written the most wonderful ode to "moving out" ever written. It will, if not causing you to immediately leap up and pack your bags, jerk you to your feet to jump and dance about the room. More than a landscape of places these are poems of sharing, of love staying behind, of a tearing, numbing loss, unshakable moments against the changing backdrop of pine and desert, California to Texas, cafes to motels. Redundant moments in the poems, so perfectly reflecting a clumsy stage, redundant freely, indecision, a needle stuck in Texas. He manages to sweep together the positioning of local color and the truly versatile linking verb of goodbye, the need for solace, unknown places ahead become the comforting mother who swallows pain. By the Thirtieth Hymn "No S.O.S. exists." A heart stretched from Mississippi to Nebraska by the strong presence of love and relentless fantasy filling in the gaps. Dream, and half dream, and reality emerging together: Vermont, Manitoba, snowshoes, the loveless motel, and the ever prevailing summer. Then the Great Smoky Mountains and love arriving on a bus. The body described and traversed in a combination of geographies that sing from the page. The barage of complexities keep coming even after travel is maintained only by comparisons. The myriad images of theworld outside still getting in from the street, through the newspaper, through the job. Is it possible to live in the midst of all this and still feel? Or as the poet asks in the Fifty-eighth Hymn:

> "Is it possible, anymore, to say I love you without universal embarassment?"

But coming through it all on his feet, Charlie Walsh so beautifully prevades the rumbles of hysteria at the door and puts it for us all in Hymn Fifty-four, declaring:

> "we somehow manage smoothness most of the time."

The poet has taken you there and brought you back forever richer. *My Summer Vacation* by Charlie Walsh is a book so real, it sweats in your hands. I love it!

Maureen Owen

FOREWORD

I look at this book the way I see my own fingers. They feel their way about in certain unlit communities like Hong Kong juvenile delinquents doing acid for the first time, alone in the Yukon. Who knows how these terrors originate? Summer vacations. A male. A female. It's difficult for me, at this point, to believe I knew who wrote these hymns. I'm tempted, rightly I think, to see the author watching the Bicentennial fireworks from the steps of a fake Parthenon located in the center of our country-and-western capitol.

Last Sunday, as Gail and I were admiring the remaining architecture in the South Bronx, I felt happiness: an odd composite of travel, art, filth, love, bad news and a good library. I wish for you only the same, all of it. See you in September for the annual hunkering down to exploratory surgery, none for me thanks.

This book of hymns seems to me now a novella. The period in which it was composed coincided precisely with a time during which I forgot to remember I was just another schmuck with a mom, a dad, and a girl in a car. It was all a mistake. I was lucky. Listen to Petrarch:

May it please you to abandon hate and scorn,
Winds contrary to the life serene;
And may time spent in harming others
Be converted into some more worthy act,
Either of the body or the mind,
Into some beautiful praise,
Into some honest study:
Then here below life is good,
And the road to heaven lies open...
I go about crying: Peace, peace, peace

Charlie Walsh
The World Trade Center
Mach 15, 1977

FIRST HYMN

Basically
We are not pessimistic
No
Way
Are we pessimistic
We are, in fact, though not optimistic
Somewhat sentient
Finding the glossy in a spider web

SECOND HYMN

Goodbye world. I'll take another
of those cute drinks in a coconut. The sharks
are circling now & all that remains
is the broken sextant & a dripping photo
of a hand on a princess telephone.
The sun hurts my eyes as I bob up & down
in this B movie; four months away
from spring training, my instinct hangs
pressed in the dugout locker near Yuma. Hot
on this island, you polish
the looking glass, the monster's eye
pins me to the beautiful surf. As patrons
of Davy Jones' Bar & Grill,
we row to the stars in the Andrea Doria
satisfied, delicious, and in deep trouble.
Don't give me no more lullabies;
we hymn ourselves into a passionate world.

THIRD HYMN

for Herb Score

The city of night is a black diamond.
I am a pitcher on the mound
with a pretty good knuckle ball,
it leaves my hand.
The ball comes off the bat
It gets larger
Hits my head.
On the ground in the center of the black diamond
a hole in my eyes makes contact with the sky
Everything is pure & white & forever.
I am scared.
There will be no more apples
Service is out
The heart beats faster & faster.
I am scared.

FOURTH HYMN

St. Joseph was a man who sat his fill on a lake one night,
the moon a blossom above the treetops, the tv stations
streaking off into the woods, a new war like vintage wine
snapping at the hills of the distant future.

Back there on the donkey, a mysteriously pregnant girlfriend
threw her head back & licked at the snow.

One star seemed larger than the others. St. Joseph
wondered why people called him St. Joseph, and not just
Joseph. When he talked to that blonde chick with the wings
months ago, how was he to know he was buying the ticket for
twenty centuries of subordination?

Hell, I'm only a carpenter.

St. Joseph thought about that other country, a land whose
vitality and sheer indifference to its own beauty, since
the day the painter had come in to order an easel and, in
passing, shown him a picture of that other country,
haunted him.

Camels. Must be some Royal Caravan. There are too many
kings. Better get her out of sight. Rape's gone up.

St. Joseph seemed to his neighbors an unassuming chap,
not the sort to hang out in bars, quiet, industrious.
His children, you could be sure, would never become
juvenile delinquents. Or troublemakers.

The problem at hand, where to spend the night.

FIFTH HYMN

We wish that we could pretend to be elsewhere, taking up space
dissimilar to any usual home, perhaps on the fringes. The
doorman is aware of this sentiment as a disturbing preparation
for an event of strength, the object of which escapes not only
ethical considerations but the weather itself. We are not lost
in alternatives, we tell ourselves, we have none. Yet it isn't
the superannuated quotidian which rabbets us like meek small
change in the fists of the rich, it rather deserves a new
sexuality of definition, a lighthearted but earnest god beyond
neuter, unrepentent for the world, a true blue elsewhere of
love where i.d. cards are unnecessary to rise in the elevator shaft
towards coconut trees, small snacks, a great baseball inning, one
final one, moving easy. Who is the river across whom the
unbelieved Christopher carries our baby ideas, we stop off for
a drink, in the middle of winter, the deskclerk reading Penthouse,
the fish are jumping, you are the necklace which fuses lightning
to my heart by holding the door open. It is, it is imaginable.

SIXTH HYMN

The girl is polishing her fingernails
in high school, the boy resists arrest
near Prague, monkeys move on deck &
splash themselves crossing an imaginary
latitude. Peace roses surface at
two hundred yards as Bengali mothers breast
feed their young, in a baseball stadium
with artificial turf a wad of tobacco
touches ground, the porpoises cresting
in the Black Stream, another dwarf
signs up for the "new german film." North
of Whitehorse, large chunks of ice crease
early morning rapids, a flower vendor
shouts to the cop on Welfare Island,
busses steamroll in the night, the banyon
tree swells, children scream at the movies
in Montevideo. A man defecates on a mountain
not far from Manila, another makes love to
his girlfriend from behind in Kamchatka,
airplanes line up at Dulles, a guy loses
his shirt in Marseilles, the medical student
falls behind in Auckland. There is no
diagnosis, no forgotten moments, the heart is
on the wheel, a pudding cooks, love
like nothing at all.

SEVENTH HYMN

I (unintelligible) you. A distinct
quality of light donates its time
towards (unintelligible) and passion. I wear
the bottoms of my trousers (garbled)
out to limit out, pass on (unintelligible) passion, a few friends
into the (erasure) you.
For example, from a song
(unintelligible) only free & easy
but impossible conceptual actual (unintelligible)
at all.
This is January. The wind hangs on your wall cadmium cobalt
(splice) soft quotidian
the true everywhere north light (unintelligible)
real (unintelligible
like there with you & to go so beyond

(blank)

EIGHTH HYMN

You are in my imagination but you are asleep
I think, at your house. Dreams where lemons
roll off bronze roofs into the grocery bags
being delivered to diplomats. Addis Abbaba
possibly although a more realistic locale
appreciates legs one of your strong suits, say
Bogota when the leaves are falling, May. So
they cross over in sleep, those legs, against
the sheets I am against employment especially
night employment since my legs, not on welfare,
like to be crossed over. You can see I am a
Christian. And awake. And at work. 3 a.m. but
the ambassador wanted tangelos, he was wounded
in the Tet offensive & they help him recover. He's new
in this dream and it would crush him to know, perhaps
the lemons, so perfect rob roy, did not realize
Bolivia is landlocked. Your mouth is slightly
open. your car is a Comet. Your pinto beans
are soaking. In South America, where even the
earth is unstable, insomnia is very common. People
will do anything to snatch sleep from the jaws of
life. Arson. Divorce. Shoplifting. Baseball. Anything.
For instance, I am a banana today. No one likes to
sleep with bananas, I mean they're nice to look at
but you get the feeling they should be out looking
for a job or something. What a terrible reminder.
Our legs are all tangled up by now in the factory,
mestizo skyscraper rosewood legs & here comes the boss,
dragging by the ear a delivery boy carrying a grocery
bag with two lemons and a banana on top.
I have to drive them to the copshop in an el camino
Celine said all bosses eat shit there are no bosses
bananas are underemployed typewriters are dreams
etc. but my circulation is being cut off by your
imaginary legs but please
"don't move them."

NINTH HYMN

You are painting naked on Union Avenue with the wind
    & the rain a radio spinach Young Lust comic books
Two select-a-career match covers what's left of a half
    dozen navel oranges a lavender/coldsfoot roll your
Own roach letters from your mother and grandfather from
    friends from Australia ideas for more paintings a
Floodlight aimed at the canvas clothes from Goodwill
    noise out of downstairs the front door locked across
The street men playing cards buying beer magazines tomato
    paste toilet paper cigarettes cars passing south past
Sears vermillion chevys the Union Avenue Social Club amber
    hillmans zinc ramblers over the burnside bridge over
Water salmon steelhead a small stomach ache things to be
    accomplished in the next twelve hours Claes Oldenburg's
I am for art that unfolds like a map, that you can squeeze,
    like your sweetys arm, or kiss, like a pet dog. Which
Expands and squeaks, like an accordian, which you can spill
    your dinner on, like an old tablecloth. A man in his
Twenty-eighth year with fingerprints a bathrobe teeth which
    hurt at times parents 2000 miles east some knowledge of
Historical dates such as 841, 1066, 1789, April 30, December 7
    an interest in photo-reproduction love for movies a wandering
Eye as the result of eleven year old touchdown into raspberry
    bush Romance by Conrad & Ford apricot nectar Conquistador
By Cecil Taylor The Best of the Supremes a smallish bunion on
    the left foot letters words paragraphs pages from
Mothers brothers corporations outfits lawyers senators nail
    clippers garbanzos Ajax Kleenex the remnants of a cold fingers
On the keys of a Facit Baldwin Trois Gnossiens by Satie four
    eleven four twelve and ten seconds twenty six-sev-eight-nine
Seconds leap year in the morning stars two days past full
    moon typing the x in the statement part of the Ninth Hymn
Lucky unlucky prone to broken arms bashed in vent windows
    surprising checks and money orders a growing love
Almonds rose hips legs hair shoulders eyes Rexroth Whalen Burroughs
    Dream of the Red Chamber Sorrentino roast beef very hot bath
An occasional need to be in another universe like I said
    in the statement typing an x sometimes I don't feel
Like a human being at all everything is air & colour & motion

& temperature & wetness & pressure & decibles & altitude
& the shape of your back as you bend with your brush & green paint
for a fraction of time & I feel like cotton & I feel
Like a hieroglyphic in a dark pyramid & I feel like George & like
Nancy & Mary & Ken & Stephen & Suzanne & Martha & Charlie like
Like I said the letter x in the animal, so abused, so ancient, the ox

TENTH HYMN

Ten thousand miles as the bird flies from Shanghai
I want to go north with you
and east and west and south. To stand on
cliffs and sleep in the ateliers
of wise men covered with honeysuckle anywhere
around the globe. "We can dance
beneath the diamond sky with one hand
waving free," in Turkey, New Zealand,
Maine or the Keys. You can sit on my face
geography, with your relief maps & bird
migrations & uranium ores & bauxite deposits
& your indigenes scattered from pole to pole
like multicolored dots like me.

I guess it's because I'm a sagittarius
I guess it's because you're a gemini
I guess it's because we're six months to the day apart
I guess it's because complacency is a drag
So let's load up the Mercedes-Benz
So let's go pick up some food stamps for Colby cheese on the way
So let's float across the Atlantic & Pacific
So let's take a trip on the B & O RR

Fauna & Flora of the World, give us pancakes
of landscape every new morning
let us make love a lot in your industrial backlash
kiss me & kiss her & stamp our traveling shoes
with wonder

ELEVENTH HYMN

filling the space

your body

is the ink in my pen

we move across the page together
insiders

alive at last!

So the rent isn't paid

So the man is looking for someone with your name

the stars trip—

ped over themselves to be out

tonight, for you

scorpio full moon

pocatello

TWELFTH HYMN

Moving into California
                                                            like
invading the world Life Magazine promised
                              hang gliding
from Tamalpais to San Quentin
                                                            artichokes
From Fort Ord to Salinas
                              facing the orient
the promise of tomorrow today: Orange County
                                                            motorcycle gangs
the Berkeley Museum with too many
                              Hofmanns
does the Los Angeles River really exist?
                                                            Someone is making
dough hand over fist here
                              & not East Oakland
could be Clint Eastwood or Bob Hope
                                                            Manson or Coppola
Nixon who can tell in California where
                              Oklahoma
freaked out wearing Fredericks of
                                                            Hollywood
where zen surfers screw dolphins in backyard
                              hot tubs
on acid drinking kelp brewer's yeast papaya
                                                            milk shakes
fingering mood rings jesus pamphlets moonies
                              but
also the best minds etc. love the attitude
                                                            await the earthquke
hike the Sierras Bodega Bay around the Santa Cruz
                              Mts. for mushrooms
air love light exercise peace quiet scenery
                                                            I can't resist
even San Jose has its good points
                              I'm here with you

we take a sauna, the therapy pool, buy a book at Shakespeare, watch
                                                                        Charlie Chan
how can we ever leave it for good?
                                    Geoff
& Laura, Steve, Kathy, Summer, Yumiko who doesn't
                                                                        live here?
after Oregon, sunshine and somewhere in the woods
                                    the lost
body of Lew Welch.   I hymn for you, Lew, in the
                                                                        promised land.
California, we feed on your produce.
                                    Take care.
Under rare gale winds up Palo Colorado Canyon our
                                                                        tent maintains.
Through the telescope at one end of a large land mass:
                                    Hearst Castle.

3
3
3

THIRTEENTH HYMN

The desert at Zuni is covered with snow
An old man waves by the side of the road, the deaf symbol
    for ever, the human symbol for hitchhike
whites sell turquoise in the co-op
government issue pre-fab houses stretch to the sunset
    adobe many years ago
Gallup New Mexico Thunderbird Wine
yesterday such a lovely elevation in the front seat, the temperature was
    dropping rapidly en route from the Canyon to First
    Mesa, so warm inside with the radio on, blue corn
Tortilla. I have a dream about my daughter in the Cactus
    Motel, she-who-smiles-a-lot hit by a car,
Wind out of four corners, antelope dusk
Abandoned towns do not belong to the U.S.A., taking black &
    white shots of gone stores, will it storm?
For the first time in two weeks, your infection disappeared, we make
    love frontally in the Duke City, Charlie's kids up early
    watch cartoons next to the bed as we softly do it over
Hold close under blankets Heckle & Jeckle

I look at you for an instant as Anne cuts my hair at 8000 feet
    first time in six years
An indian's car won't start near the cafe on Central, we
    drive on chile relleno I know I love you in the
Streetlights "Fifteen miles east of Laredo right six or seven
    look for buttons on low hills

FOURTEENTH HYMN

We are in Texas now, the dust filling the cadillacs
buried near Amarillo, ghosts of entire armies
& wetbacks riding tumbleweeds up against the barbed
wire desert, the huge wheeled water lines
to hose down sage in Deaf Smith County under oil
derricks radio towers signs for Real Mex Food.
You barely murmur as we scarf down hundreds
of miles from Juarez to Johnson City on pecans
and chocolate milk. You are so quiet leaning
against the Arizona Cafe when I light your Kent
golden Light, the laundromat across an unpaved
fifth avenue mixing panties with my L.A. Thrift store
Roy Jefferson t-shirt next to the dried out Hotel Longhorn.
Or you are angry in Austin
waiting in the car while I search for my songwriting
buddy among all the college students & pizza
joints & bookstores. Later, in the St. El
Motel you won't talk you write a poem
about lost men who needed you for a moment
in a bar or by the side of the road on this trip
how you didn't give them "that quick release"
how you hate all the bourgeoise shit in this capital
city anyway. There is something mysterious
you never tell me becoming friends again in Houston
sinking several inches a year, over-civilized
sevnteen golf courses inside the city limits but tons
of excellent art. How unhappy
you seem stopping for a burger on Galveston
island when all you wanted was a picnic, light,
on the beach & to be still near the gulf
with me tonight but I do not know. I do not know
what you think these days
with the sun and billy's song Hands
On the Wheel sung by Willie all day to a night full
of enormous vistas and vague untouchable ranchos.

FIFTEENTH HYMN

Alone in Mississippi of all the states
have I felt, as the water mocassin
curls into sunlight, a material growth,
the brand new word in a rich organic still life.
Like pure oxygen floating about an amusement
park, our bodies sailed under the waves
into which poured, unfortunately, all the sewage
from beachfront urbanization. The Gulf
of Mexico, I could swim in the name for a month!
Or as one local sweet potato farmer put it,
Hurricane Camille slamming into his house, '69,
as he hid in the bathtub under a large piece of plywood
with the corn whiskey "If they don't stop
fucking with space travel they'll kill us all!"

So pecan trees and insect bayous and boondock
guitarists with songs about someone's ex-wife & a gun;
since Palm Sunday the sun has directed my tongue
into the black curly hair of your crotch
to lick the interiors of all your organs
with four i's, four s's, two p's and an m.

do not know you don't tell me in Texas
you act as if it's unimportant in Texas
egrets sail over the refinery in Port Arthur, Texas
we are totally silent leaving Texas

SIXTEENTH HYMN

From where I sit
it's Thursday April 15, 1976 at 2:30 p.m.
A spell ago I made some eggs with pimento
cheese, peppers, an onion, herbs. A slight
breeze waffles across the homemade wood furniture
mildly twisting a barely bruised magnolia
blossom. The flying squirrel sails from his living
room tapestry perch across my line of view
into the kitchen for a snack of Velveeta & water
before Celia returns with the groceries.
Rob lies asleep in the hallway, Joe is working
on his Ninth National/International Sculpture Conference
article for Feathersword. Laddie pulls up on a chopper,
we share a few numbers, everyone forgets
to ask him to bring a coleman lantern
so we can spear flounder tonight in the gulf.
Whatever, we'll see him later. Tomorrow it's a
cabin cruiser out to Cat Island.
Everything is stuffed and satisfying.

From where I sit
you can see framed in the doorway
three complete stairs, and part of another,
which lead, behind a dusty transom, to
the landing I know exists where yesterday you threatened
to shout "rape" after we made love, laughing.
From there, the top of the stairway, if you make
a right, lies on the bed, uncovered, your
sleeping body. I see how the space looks
from seeing, hours before, when I asked
you felt sleepy, if you cared for eggs or grass you didn't.

From where I sit
as I turn through a coffee table Lakes
Of The World, a souffle of light
attaches itself, in order, to
Erie, Superior, Great Slave & Victoria flipped about
by the hickory leaves on the other side
of old beveled windows.
There is around everything this afternoon

the easy sough of a lack of immediate needs
to be met.   We all dream softly for now
& only later, on a trip to buy po'boys, will
my desire transform into conversation.
These moments alive.

SEVENTEENTH HYMN

Traveling alone through Selma, Alabama on Good Friday
at three in the afternoon, the backwoods highways
lined on both sides with houses looking like
erased Walker Evans' photos, inhabited by monks to a god
that was run over, drunk, by a good old boy.
Alone, that is, traveling. My eyes hanging out
of my head like clumps of baking soda in unmixed biscuits
cooked too low for too long.   Needing
decompression badly, anointed for the sacrifice,
belly up in a fifteen year old pure white auto
stiffening towards every telephone pole I pass.
Alone except for gas stations, men in wasted striped apparel
pace out to my rolled down window, lean down.
My total vision souped down to a strip of asphalt, the toothless
bearded managers, the pre-war coke machines like emulsified
blood against the flaking green paint
behind thin glass doors.   Alone except for the Alabama State
Police.   Alone in the front seat of a car
trying to remember your voice as I held you & you said
"is for the best, Charlie
"is for the best
"is for the
"is for
"is

I know who he is.   In Birmingham a sign
for Karate School.   A thousand miles south

of my gravesite doing seventy alone towards a new
home twenty gulping down air
plucked by Nashville from the vast interlocking
thoroughfares sallow in the shadow of tomorrow.
My hands shake, my brain as weak as ice.
Swallow me, mother.
love has broken.

EIGHTEENTH HYMN

The lost poems are lost, you cannot find them
in any time zone with a warrant for their arrest. I am
the first line in a lost poem
that is unable to begin but begins
anyway, crosshairs in the mouth of the invisible man:
the moon is full and the refrigerator empty.
You are in the delta with your new lover, the sign
in mathematics signifying change. It's an adjustable
world like vaudeville that yanked us together,
two holograms interesecting in the afternoon behind gauze
curtains for some months and that's that. I cried. It tore
me up. We didn't expect it.
I think of you now as beautiful as you will ever be &
the world equals bricks trees the noise of cars clothes lines
neighbors trashcans birds a woman walking down the alley white
levis orange blouse today I photographed
a burn-out Chinese Laundry near Music Row against a pale
azure sky, an old black man in a red baseball cap
in the parking lot of the Bland Casket Co. said the insurance
never paid off. The three owners found it impossible,
he said, to separate their interests.
I am becoming, in black & white, the last line
sailing every summer for the lost poem of Europe,
my grandparents are all as dead as doorknobs.
You tell me you are unhappy & confused & just want to paint.

NINETEENTH HYMN

Where does the noise appear to come from? The noise!

The sun and the night have captured me.
In my dreams you have become a magnetic
force which keeps the car humming
& the soles of the feet pressed to hot desert salt.
No one knows why I walk.

Like the hymns of the ants who carry food
across eastern europe for the mourners
of an unforgiveable autism, my heart
is a ragged fish in a drained bayou, as blind
in your hands as my wisdom teeth
under a landfill being bulldozed
into the powder which will power me nowhere.

TWENTIETH HYMN

There is a dream formed by a Cadillac convertible
cruising West Texas in the detritus of two hundred
million lives. The bumps on Eldorado
are early warning signs of a cancer too embracing
not to be immortal. It is. We are.
In the frozen heat of the dust-filled coma, wake me up!
The vehicle moves us
over underground oilfields like broken glass
falling twenty-seven
stories to a parking lot. No one will
live through a dream. Some redneck
motherfucker will plug you from 300 meters
in Odessa at the precise moment
I present you with a panatomic photo
of a slamon colored wayside flower snapped up miles before
by a tourist. I am slumped
over the steering wheel writing this,
someone somewhere listens to the horn
and watches effortlessly the twin beams
of the headlights highlight the deserted fog.

TWENTY-FIRST HYMN

Whittled down from the various diseases of the world
paring the marble to the interior form itself
enormous changes eating themselves, my fifty odd
years walk in your direction, by your side
as the river winds nowhere, a brazen intaglio.
I'll be placing bets on Kentucky Derby Day
as I am today, in half a century
on a porch screened from the consecutive generations
of flying insects while the rockets fall at warp
factor five unto a United States rich with a quarter
millenium of chestnuts, merkins and killer bee honey.

Will you be there to hare a mint julep
in the seventh heaven of the arab cosmology
after

Emerald
    White Silver
        White Pearl
            Ruby
                Red Gold
                    Yellow Jacinth
will you bed down, lover, with me in the

Shining Light?

TWENTY-SECOND HYMN

From the assorted proofs of God
wielded like monkey wrenches upon
the minds of medieval monks
they left, unwittingly, you out.
I haven't. At 31,000 feet over North Platte,
Nebraska anything is possible:
below me, at this moment 24,000,000 TVs
draw juice from the indifferent American
river systems for the rerun of a soap opera
in which Mary Alice wrecks the family country
squire because Dan tried to make it with Jenny
over the holidays and besides, she might,
she's been told, need a transplant.
Dust to dust, I am in a pressurized cabin
speeding away from you at 550 m.p.h.
Sister Mary Gerald addressed the first graders
at Sacred Heart, "The briefest glimpse of god
in all His glory would prove fatal
to a mere human being." Linda Lovelce
was in that classroom & so was
I. Hiking with you
up the Little Sur River on Passion Sunday
smoking virginia slims under redwood & eucalyptus
trees, I began to see what she'd been getting at.
Today is the birthday of my heart.

TWENTY—THIRD HYMN

The messengers have arrived on the local from Aqueduct
with dead fish and new left ventricles. I'm on the portable
massage table without love, only documentation.

The latest release from my mind is a killer,
looking straight at it, an intelligence
no cabby would consider a legitimate fare.

The trees and cafes and whodunits I want
to share with you are empty clips
in a carbine held by a mute boy soldier
who pisses on shrubbery late at night on Paris Island.
This is a century without islands!

Like furniture teased into a brilliance
its objectivity can never hope to repay,
my possibility is a green tomato on your monkey wood
cutting board. These are the various hairs
on my body, this is a photograph
fifteen years old, a cub scout reading the Idiot.

My mom will die. My dad will die.
Everyone I know even casually is taking it easy, moving
around during the different hours, enjoying
what activites they can, an
interesting cross-section of engaged humans.
Words are as useless to me as our absence.

When I told you the story on Lake Pontchartrain
of Apollinaire's one-winged birds who only
flew in pairs, what, you asked,
happened to the extras?

TWENTY—FOURTH HYMN

I am the residue of whom I was on the day
we met in the museum, climbing into a future
now the past, ten thousand miles, Bolinas
to Biloxi on the white sands, the bayous, two
deserts, a gulf and an ocean. We write
letters to each other now from opposite ends
of the south. Carve buffalo hunting tableaux
on the doors of rusted Chevolets under
kudzu vines and spanish moss. Seventy-five
leagues away, I imagine your life among the shrimpers
& pipefitters to be a white meteor
splattering the hard edge air where blues were
born. Up here I do the Jake Walk
with barflies & pretent you were never mine.
I become, though, my own guru in the end, saying,
"From before I ever laid eyes on you
it led to you, a scenic tour astonishing
in the complexity of its geographies,
bewildering in the scope of its personal danger."

TWENTY-FIFTH HYMN

Somebody is shaking up middle Tennessee
with these flashes and rain
and loud noises.
In a little green castle not far from the beach
a lover plays guitar for you,
it's been a nice day. Five hundred miles to the northeast
under an 80% chance of showers I listen to Art Blakey
& his Jazz Messengers wishing I were Mercury
speeding south to you from the early morning sky over
Hudson Bay. I look at myself in the mirror. It's late
spring. By the time the snow melts
at higher elevations, I'll know where I stand.
Like an all day sucker left on the hood
of a black Packard, midsummer Oklahoma,
where flying saucers may once have been sighted,
someone awaits your love. Such brief
experiences, then nothing!

TWENTY-SIXTH HYMN

The vintners can't agree
on the year of your birth, whether
green makes a more suitable bottle
or am I blue?
                                    Take your clothes off, lover, for me
wherever you are and with whom.
Your letters fill me with the ineffable passion
of the first flower to grow on Venus.   Fuck
the solar system, I want to say it
                                                                    right
every time, a breathless way you've taught
me to go through life
merely a train, a Louisville & Nashville
running under the pillow in that position
you liked so last month.   It has been five now,
five months we've known each other on the summer
solstice, a night I'll spend missing you as I watch,
my final glass of wine
                                                 almost downed
two dancers neck to Roy Buchanan
this twenty-seventh year.

Tomorrow I will send in more boxtops to Mississippi
where you've been advertised
                                                            as the prize

TWENTY-SEVENTH HYMN

Another day has passed into the lexicon
of passages we will never speak about:
the weather existed, a cop was killed
forty kilometers from his home, some teams
won their games and some lost. From
an alley which runs into the alley I live
on, the sound of a dog in pain. age.
bad owners. worms. spoiled fish. It
could be anything but it's us kissing
and then you kissing someone else.

In Juarez once, a mexican boy came over
in front of the bench we were necking on
(it was a plaza in early April) whipped out
several dozen popsicle sticks, criss-crossed
them, smiled, and lit them on fire. Twenty
girl drummers in uniform were marching
around a statue covered
with birdshit. Maybe 10 a.m. local time.
these things mean very little

as tonight, I share Galliano with the woman
who gave bith to me 27 years ago, I wonder
who you will give birth to in the next thirteen,
will there be deer parks? My favorite horse
won the Derby this year, cleanly, but you
were as far from me then as you are now,
as personally inaccessable as the culture
which ritualized psychotropics millenia
ago, Ah...love, Ah...art, Ah...the senses
Wrap me up & place me in your arms today!

TWENTY-EIGHTH HYMN

I am in a sealed pine box
carried through the alleys of your love
on the shoulders of hot, unfriendly dice.

It is cold in here. The rain has started.
The prayer wheel is spinning now, lover,

pounding my heart into sardines.
I hate adverbs, I want to be immaculate, write lines like

this,

all human experience
tending in me towards you

All this space!

I have no home.

Someday we will live with the flamingoes

TWENTY-NINTH HYMN

The city runs smack into midnight
turning a new day with packs of wild
dogs attacking children in Philadelphia
under mercury vapor boulevards
only the distant hum of disco.
Sunday's a full moon, my poems
disappearing in Kingdom City,
Missouri I feel nervous about you. Every 12 year old
wears chains & dreams of Kiss
or one of the Tubes, the trees
are limpid with summer, my finger
slides across Deuteronomy
with hysteria like the hopelessness of the blonde
I'm holding comes despite her Silva Mind Control
Certificate. Wanting to see colors right now.
A man of letters is telling another honored
gentleman in the dark pine booth of the bar the roots
of Chinese civilization: Oh, yellow soil
patrilineal descent, a written language that is early
& inscrutable but necessary to foreign merchants.
Hundreds are enjoying turkey pot pies tonight
as I think about you with love & too much
hair in my mind. there is barking,
the barometer is flaccid but swollen: good weather,
in some ways we are indulged by the world.
I think of a moment we spent in the cold atop
the deepest canyon on the continent, tomorrow
I will scribble the words on a paper napkin
to a song without lyrics:
"There is, I suppose, a certain desperation."

THIRTIETH HYMN

My bed kicks me out of bed when you're not in it. We go
fifteen rounds under protest together, a few milion feathers
and 97¢ worth of trace minerals searching under ourselves for
you, it's no use. Without you, I stay up late eating Dijon
Mustard, listening to Art Tatum, reading Tu Fu. My brain
begins its half-life balanced on the seesaw of how or how not
you've changed. Do your lips twist up when you smile? Are
your feet any softer on the Mississippi clay? My bed cannot
know. My bed is a new armament invented by a crazed government
for the pacification of bronze age urges. I deposit myself
nightly in it with you in mind. Your body, it tells me,
is somewhere else. Somewhere, on your 27th birthday, with
someone else. My bed is all hands lost on a spice ship
flying an anonymous flag in the fourteenth century minus
your limbs of gold. No S.O.S. exists.

THIRTY-FIRST HYMN

I'm walking down Broadway here
near the river like prune juice
moving through the tubes of a rock star on stage
it's impossible to inhabit cities without you.
I keep imagining an ocean that's blue
like the white of your skin, that enters as
a melting glacier five miles up, winds
its way through autumn in New England
to fill the bathtub we could be making love in
tonight, a long distance phone call, enough
money to forget money, your hand on my
heart, my mouth on your neck of necks.
"I am a dying man," I tell the Jesus freaks we
have only fifty years to get even with god.
I go through motions, kiss the city,
keep busy. My brother, who really likes you,
tells me to forget you, the bottom line
where my existence turns into a flash cube
sold to an alien on a deserted street corner

located where a meteor killed a rabbit
and three insects 8000 years ago.
Even now, my eyes wander desperately
over the landscape it is possible to share
with you.

THIRTY-SECOND HYMN

We live in splendour now
  with the airconditioning chilling
    the hell out of the urn
to be used for our children's ashes; the mts.
  are still white and blue rivers tumble
    down our dreams like picnic spots
on the road across the Yukon where we hang
  out the bigtop to dry in the residual dark.
    I wish I knew what I had for lunch today.
It was frozen, it was probably made
  by the mother of three in a townlet
    governed & commented upon by civilized functionaries,
I ate it in the panelled veneer quiet
  of the Central Coffee Shoppe. It's difficult
    not to be positive about this use of space, to
not say that poets who look for the 1000 years
  of peace are hard evidence already of its intrusion
    into the masterpiece of homelife this century.
To go fishing is to reject Pax Americana
  with its tame mustangs & graduated tax scale
    unless it can be seen as a "vacation."
I love this country and I love you
  but they are incompatible. Our secret pleasures
    subvert the scheme & the poor natives
who turn into the oil to run our autos
  have nothing better to do than feed
    off the decay what we were born into
daily becomes. To stay alive will soon
  be all. TV prepares us; given that,
    how might I hum the retired word?

THIRTY-THIRD HYMN

The Quick Storm

The wind cracks across banana trees
in countries we have never been, the bicyclist
in orange races through the alleys
"Le Mistral, le Mistral." Oh chimney sweeps
don't drown rise up salute the perfervid air,
the barometer exhausts itself. Wheels
of our mind, you are
the only instruments we can land on.

Clouds which eat spider webs for breakfast
nudge the whores even closer to their doorways.
Young people gallop home in their pintos
and morris minors, it's all so
flexible so statuesque so jack-in-the-boxsh this
thing less than a typhoon
more than Benjamin Franklin could understand.

the naked farmgirls of Kansas are still naked,
Martin Heidegger & Johnny Mercer have died,
a neo-plastic Zeus has me barely dry under the eaves
glad to have known you
even gladder to be in bed with you tonight
though I'm not & you're 844,000 yards away.
This storm, however, moves towards Memphis
& James Earl Ray.

The trees are now like coffins, the mockingbirds
are no longer silent. Everyone,
in Chinese, people-people, is occupied
watching the Immigrants on television.
The temperature rises once again,
clothes continue their fightened drying
while I study your handwriting for the forecast.

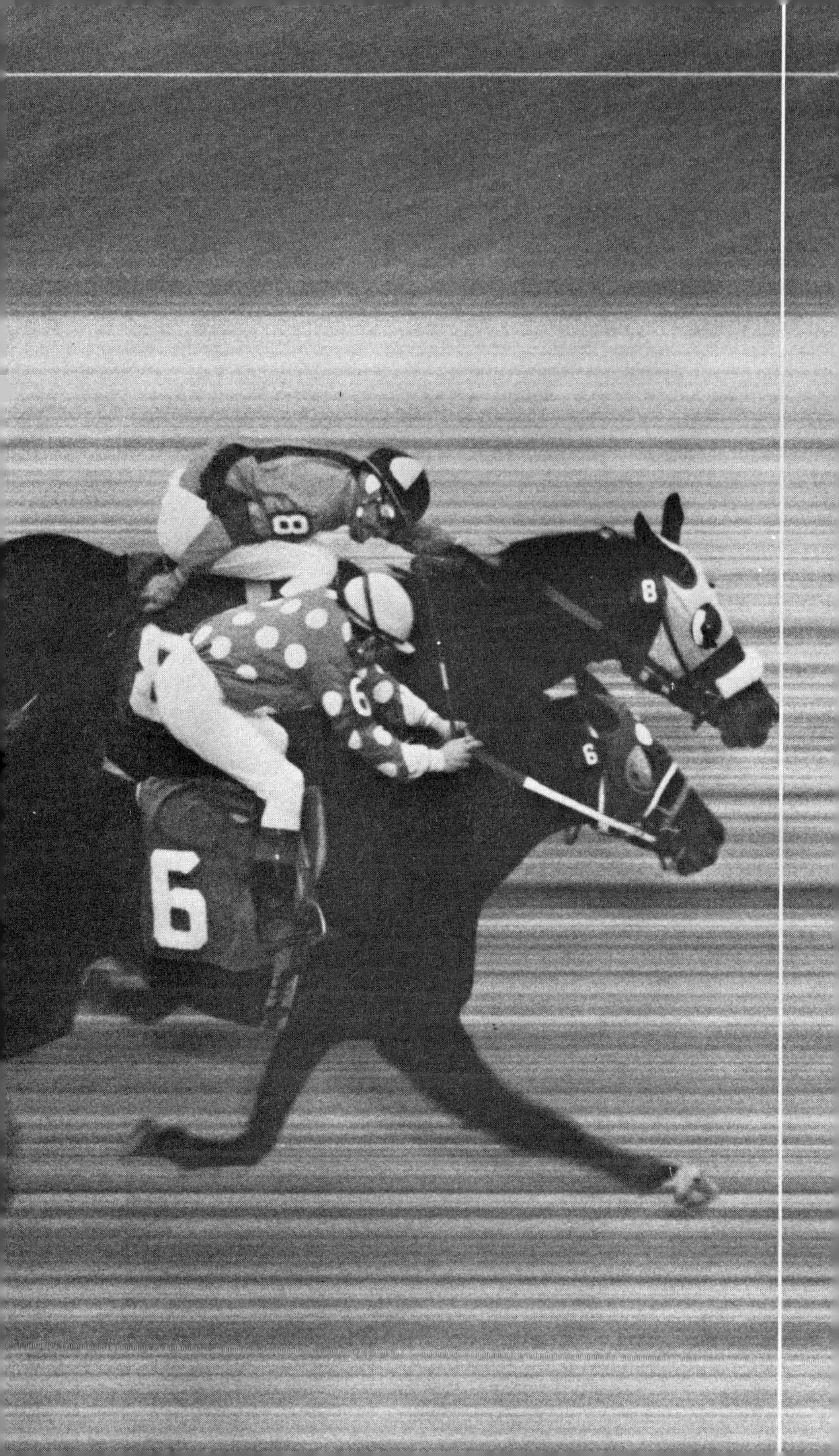
8
8
8
6
6
6

THIRTY-FOURTH HYMN

A Freedom Railroad, built by the People's Republic of
China links Tanzania & Zambia. What
keeps you where you are,
fanning yourself, broke, your thinning arm
lifted in a useless gesture against the chiggers
of inactivity? Would you like
part of my estate since I never see you?

I fall off curbs: thinking about your skin
Your thighs: I stay up all night at the age of nine.

Oh states of the south Georgia Mississippi Alabama
your houses have no roots, for two hundred years
& a war they stand on blocks
while poor men lose teeth into guitar holes on front
porches painted like faded billboards Ziggy's Bar-B-Q
Ma's Eats the rusted broken rails of the Dixie RR siding.
We work out the summer in a garbage strewn
domesticated Oz dragged out from under, by slaves &
smallpox, literate indians. I dream about you,
girlfriend & south, like twin abandoned stations
muscled against the heat.

Everywhere the weddings & funerals of a land
which claws us into paradise
slowly, against the combined will of the elements
& our own nervous misdirections.

THIRTY-FIFTH HYMN

We are passing into history at an astonishing
pace. Peace is impossible
for the locomoted engines which rust
in the rains of a barefoot deep south,
how we've known each other now for half
a year, pensionless, in bed with others,
there is no straight man to bounce off of here

WILD HORSES DROP DEAD IN UTAH

FROM MYSTERIOUS CAUSE

I grow close to the furniture in my room
I take baths.
The sun evens its score with me
as you wash what clothes you have left
in someone else's machine.

Correct me if I'm wrong. I'm underlining
the word "love" in one of your letters, automobiles
chase each other around, pomegranates contain
more vitamin C than the dying Pacific.

To be only in the arms of a saxophone,
a pillow to the new world
out of brass cutting new reeds each day
who needs the french foreign legion at 27
I'm a regular guy.

You kneel in the tub in an inch of water six months ago
& wash your long hair under the faucet:
I will always love you for it
deeply, does anyone know how it all turns out?

Perhaps you should spell it
to protect the kids.

THIRTY-SIXTH HYMN

Your browned boy ground itself
into the eyeglass where the world exposed
what was in my pockets to love
& that heady feeling which comes over
men and women. In High Times
they call it leather, sex and mushrooms,
in my mind it is ripening cantaloupes & honeydews
like questionmarks at the end of the line
"Will I ever see you again?????"

THIRTY-SEVENTH HYMN

The insects are biting you now; your skin,
which is the dust sifting through the fingers
of next century's natives, receives impersonal
mutilations from an air force of one day old fliers
with latinate names. My gaze focuses
beyond the screen of someone else's bedroom
on a sleek black mustang across
the street with a sticker price of $4395 F.O.B.
Detroit. Leonard Woodcock is on TV
with a Jimmy Carter button as I think suddenly
of my hands coming out of the mailbox
minus a letter from you. Everywhere there are
citizens drinking fermented grains to the health
of new-made friends, my BANQUET dinner
boils in its sealed plastic pouch, Veal
Parmigiana 33¢, I'm getting laid
regularly, three friends in Oil City, Pa.
killed themselves within two weeks, unemployed
or factory worker or gas station attendant,
for a month now I've barely
heard your voice in my sleep. I try, I concentrate
on looking at my hands in the middle of a dream
to consciously locate you. My dream:
"I think you

are thinking about someone you love."
Each day I awake a night closer
to an ancient city, now uninhabited,
where the syllables of your name are chanted
by the impaired, winging it.

THIRTY-EIGHTH HYMN

Seven Crystals in the Radio I Hear

1. This could be a sonnet snuck across the borders
   to call it love, moving backwards from Yugoslavia
   towards the Italian refugee camps, apolitical,
   almost agrarian in intent, some sort of strange
   organic fix that zooms in on you behind the iron curtain
   of other hands and other legs to melt the skin
   I am crawling out of in my need to touch your nipples
   and smoothe your hair and neck with your mind.

2. The wind races the moon
   around my neighborhood to the swivel
   of people over thirty rocking on porches
   no longer hell bent
   but not yet comfortable with this year's
   new shows. Some redhead sings
   a plaintive country air
   as my landlord, a Baptist preacher,
   calculates this month's take and a sniper
   in Wichita assasinates total strangers
   from the downtown Holiday Inn.

3. These events move
   in their own form.
   Forget the sports pages!

4. This could be a villanelle snuck across the borders
to call it love, how your body has become a legend
touching mine and shines like a polished flower
across my entire dream in this relentless summer.
To be jaded by everything but you.

5. Nanda Devi Ohlmsted, 22 year old daughter of
the famous American mountaineer, William Ohlmsted,
perished today while climbing the moutain her father
named her after. Altitude was given as the reason for
her death. Her father, climber of Everest, accompanied
her on the attempted assault. 22,000 feet.

6. You can be a war in which there is no
winning side. You can be the gem
worn around the ankle which crushes me.

7. If only you weren't so far away
& with another guy

THIRTY-NINTH HYMN

I am not in Majorca and not with you,
two negatives which combine to form the positive
of a place in line at the pawnbrokers
where they offer 10% for my prosthetic brain.
From afar, the ballads seemed quite compelling
before I ran into the drunk with my pickup
striding towards the Cafe la Renaissance once
you disappeared. Rolling in my sweet baby's
arms has left me ravaged
almost impolite. I'm ready for L.A.
& its beautiful artificial palms.
This tour lasted longer than they promised.
Fringe benefits hang from my months without you
like baby powder on the body of a frightened one year old,
his folks laid out on the lawn under incoming mortars.

FORTIETH HYMN

Your body alters itself over five hundred miles
into a country I forgot to buy a visa for. I am in Vermont
or Manitoba buying snowshoes with two dollar bills

                    at an impossible altitude. Several thousand atomic bombs
                    lie armed for us under fields of soybeans grown
                    by the "organic method." the desk was heavy, you

write, the one you dragged down the RR tracks
from a junked homestead; I write this on an old oak
rolltop in a house abandoned by you a couple

                    weeks ago. As I complete a forced march up the side
                    of a slushy south face, it comes to me: clearly
                    this is winter, you may dream about me

but I've checked into the Loveless Motel
for the duration. We are dirty with amour
& they tell us the script calls for deprivation testing.

                    Remarkably, I remember your body as, to borrow a phrase, "my
                    heart's garden," my writing hand is nailed to the wall with
                    your postcards, my eyes wheel about dizzy with you while

I suck plastic. He didn't realize, they say about me,
that the potential energy of height without sunglasses
pushes on into the entropic kinetics of the mass paralysis.

FORTY-FIRST HYMN

The affectation of movement
            traced by the ink in these lines
moves me. Sunlight & butterflies
            etch the surface of the pool
below the waterfall about a boy
            from Princeton sunbathing
on an orange air-mattress a budweiser can
            moves up and down on his chest.
Soon the clouds from Hurricane Dotty
            will call it a day 1100 miles west
of the eye in the state of Tennessee.

Surrounded by overhanging hawthornes
            "When will you take off
your clothes for me
            again in the luxury to which we grew used?"

FORTY-SECOND HYMN

I welcome you to the heart you left disheveled
with fondness & love. Your long bus ride
is over, your short hairs are wet with what
we hope will be the end of anxiety, at least
for us, at least for awhile. The skies
ascend from the earth all day, erector
sets powered by pressure differentials like
the eyes I look into when you first see me.
With cherry cheese and wine from Milan
we can, we hope, begin to wind
on a diamond needle, moving true north. Love
isn't definitive or just or even merciful as we threaten
its borders but it is a range
on which the finest animals "walk with beauty"
towards the inevitable desserts.
It's crazy how de rigeur the avoidance of happiness
has become. This is no Bergman film.
I only wish not to say I love you
because the evidence will transcend linguistic form.

FORTY-THIRD HYMN

I want to complete my stories
climbing beyond the new science & play
to the biologic wildness I feel for you.
Paragraphs of temporary insanity look me up
at 3 a.m., I throw a pinch
of salt over my shoulder and love you again.
There is no plausible punctuation
to surround the remarks of my tongue, oh
apostrophes of every moment! You
say it and then I say it, "Our motors
are running with a remarkable passion
this morning in the Great Smoky Mountains."
There is nothing else today, nor need
there be.

FORTY-FOURTH HYMN

in
these
mountains
I
don’t
care
who
wins
what
war

Clouds cannot obscure the bulge in my bathing
suit. My veins are seven miles of ink stylizing
the world.

FORTY-FIFTH HYMN

The smell of your body is money
passing through the hands of my dreams
in which the beautiful women of the world
line up to applaud the taste of your body.
The money will pay for sundries, it buys
Sunday morning on Lake Como, immortality,
radishes, a touch of geranium lake in a promise
anyone green yesterday. The taste of you
brings artists on the dole to their knees.
Ruby lasers transmit your smell in an instant
to the far corners of outer space where indigo
leaves fall, twisting, from heaven to earth
in a matter of seconds like the dazzle of police
sirens climbing glossy black fire escapes
to rescue men, obviously, who have never smelled you
in deep rest, in the heat of summer with your ears
pinned to the wind beyond small talk.
Your smell is the luau pit where all my fires
hum themselves into songs sung by the deaf
in churches of universal good hands. Your
taste is the rosebud sleigh in Citizen Kane
wrapping up its imaginary existence under
the religious eyes of Samoans in a World War
II theatre. Whatever you do, your odor
and the overdrive you leave in my mouth
will move me across creekbed rocks to
a god I do not believe in like a tatoo discovered
on my brain by some ridiculous final agent
in a useless mechanistic ideology you alone
possess the grace to unravel for me.
I am the sole hum of a protean substance
run callously amok on the screen of a television
smashed years before by a pilloried genetic code.

7892345234567892345678923
6 RACE Nov. 7.
IRROR
IMAGE

FORTY-SIXTH HYMN

The tragedy of their lives
The way busses take them to their death
And Cancer and love and jealousy
Ulysses a mound of dirt somewhere
In Greece, another civil war
We all try to make ends meet
With bluster, guns, sentiment
How lovely these visits we spend
With each other, I love you, saying
Or the color of your eyes, what
You wear. The joy in their lives
From plain jane to exquisite pleasure
And it in all ways always undercut
Oh emotion of living. So let
The snows fill up my ears
The water buffalo step on my toes
The ancient monuments retain their tics
& have certain tender moments.

FORTY-SEVENTH HYMN

I want to wander with a woman who
notices the shortness of breath the sun has assumed
from colour alone, someone
to whom nothing is as abstract as a city street.
I can imagine roughing it with her
through small villages lifted like snapshots
from the memories of frozen corporals
but there will be intrigues
and crimes of passion before we have finished.
I never want to finish.
If we are polished off in a duel of manners
by an accidental affair not far from a ghost town
let it be said of us, "Even astrological congruence
can mean nothing given the universal wattage
of current life."
I will not be happy to pick clean
our histories in an awful gratuitous solitude.
In fact, the touch of this woman's skin
would be more than an ace bandage
on more than this man's body.

FORTY-EIGHTH HYMN

You come down on me in the Jalapeno
pepper garden like an avenging angel
on the head of the pin which holds me
together after the accident of this world.

The sun is busted by cloud police for vagrancy.
The taste of the memory of you is an ex-marine
mass murderer following me home from grammar school,
where you are never more than what I reach for
in the night when you are not there.

"Your imaginary luminosity" and I am able only
on some wierd tomorrow to kiss your ankles
and the insides of your thighs. Needing to ride
trains with you through jungles of ancient
masterpieces will never not swing the saloon
doors open to you painting in a studio
too "just so" not to be true.

The words without ancestors which numb my mouth
since I haven't the foggiest whether you're dead or alive
tonight like a Mexican knife
eat me up with all this missing-you-business
in the hot pepper garden where the reality
of decomposition sells me over the counter
for a quick vision of you, a hologram in the weeds
life on Mars does not seem to let me touch.

FORTY-NINTH HYMN

It's times like these you come to me with your lost
& found eyes & body I can see forever barefoot
across the ashes on the bosque of the Rio Grande. Your
ten fingers have curled beyond the limits of American
beauty to brush the thrushes of a thousand resurrected
experiences in exotic trees everywhere. Love has
treated you indifferently. What a city we have never
inhabited! I refuse to be romantic about your mouth
which opened my life like a can opened on the day we met
it's too much, the erratic grace you carry like lemons
fills my brain cavity with the fairytale lust of a mystic
fed only low-grade grains. As you crawl with a knife
in your teeth towards the only heart I was born with
I live only for you. Nothing casual about it,
they keep us in separate cages and I cannot
see you from here. Why literature exists.

FIFTIETH HYMN

You are on the other end of the phone in my hand
which is flesh-colored. Our words to each other race
across the deep south with the speed of death notices
to the concerned family members & just wanted to see
what y'all up to tonight. Millions intersect long
distance to order shirts, new banks, or inquire the price
of auto lubrication. We exact nothing more than the date
as if we were sympathy cards arriving, as usual, late but
better than... how to come inside you this time with more
feeling or always & you still four days away mere words.
I am going to destroy the means of instant communication
before anyone gets hurt because my fingers need to touch
the linemen who touch the means of touching you. Why were
old cars black? Am I lost for good in the white comet
you sold me for a buck?

You talking to me? You talking to me? I work in a
restaurant where everyone plays a different character.
Tomorrow to find out who I am. They tell me. Let me
kiss your ears. I am in the emergency room of my own
mental state. They want pictures, they say, I love you,
how far away hear you humming, you never sing, a voice
in a phone booth at a pre-set time, four days, okay see
you then. This time for good. This time be happy solvent
shady immaculate sober silly real. Can it be done you
talking to me? The "old college try" make it work worth
sleeping on, how does a telephone say I love you & not
come out wired.

The way you walk can walk over me. How enjoyable
it is to kiss you with the lips I've grown up with!
Is the telephone interested in language like that?
When you pick it up during the first ring after a
mile walk there is no such animal as love, only the
sun & the buildings & the people who dare to move
about. But we all do, our odd sensitivities crunch
together & hurt & feel good even have fun during
the time I am thinking of what to say to the woman
I love while you, the reader, waits.

FIFTY-FIRST HYMN

I wanted a world with romantic engines
to feed myself into, a moebius strip where images
recycle themselves like unattached proteins
kissing each other in the heart of a be-loose
concept sussed around somehow mystically
on the wheels of your sultry princessness.
You didn't quite see it that way.
Our photograph yellowed in the attic of no niagara falls
no santa catalina no costa del sol
because I had to learn that love supports
this business of existence and is not the flashy prayer
of a sprinter with translucent designs.
You taught me all this in your own way, sleeping
with others, passing out
of my life for extended gothic divorces
while I insulated myself with bandages of blondes.

To never be hoarse form the underpinnings
of our secret inclusive share of events
has proven enough to listen to haunted Moslem requiems
without jerking about like some 19th century "sensitive."
What more can I ask? There are no checkmates,
bruised cabbies may yet drop us home.

FIFTY-SECOND HYMN

In the old country
with whips cracking black carriages
through dusty orchards
my need for you would imply a duel
for favors; seconds would tick off
the correct distance & the winner would flee.
Perhaps you go with him.
Today's already cool customs
allow me to wait while you make up
your mind. To swim through summer
with my head underwater
until your lungs burst from decision.

In the new country
the leaves begin to spin into colours,
the air cools as we imagine & live
amongst the upcoming glitter of winter.
Oh opera season! We are nowhere yet
but fabulous architectures slip
their invitations under our nervous doors.
There are many times an extra touch
as you move into me with flesh & blood.
I salute the future with the past.
I hymn myself into your colorful world.

FIFTY-EIGHTH HYMN

White sheets drape in the blue sky;
in Brazil, spring has arrived. Here,
the hard tan leaves of the tulip tree
circle about and brush me
as my fountain pen moves on a civil war porch.
You are napping.
Some grizzled neighbor rough saws 2x4"s
for an unknown project, a long
fire truck passes in the sun.
Today we dropped by the unemployment &
employment offices after the purchase
of suede & black velvet jackets from the fall opening
at the Ladies of Charity Thrift Store,
good deals. You aren't talking. A letter
from your ex-lover hangs in the air, your new
employer seems to be a handsome
european. The painting you are working on
keeps slamming like a door in your face, what
I feel for you is slammed into mine.
The children are out of school now, dogs
chase each other near Granny's Snacks,
a freight to Georgia whistles. Soon
the ice cream truck will come down the road
on a song, the paper will arrive with more child
abuse stories, perhaps we'll take a swim.
These novellas continue, starving kittens show up
at our door, a scientist claims
it might be possible to reverse chromosomal breakdown,
to live, say, eight hundred years.
Is it possible, anymore, to say "I love you"
without universal embarassment? A kid
down the block plays the penny whistle flute & I think
of the Apu Trilogy but you wake, we share
a fudgsicle and touch each other lightly.
Nine/Seventy Six.

FIFTY-NINTH HYMN

Our skin touches. Outside are the large clouds
                    perspiring when I dream of you. Your hand has
paint under the fingernails, wanting you
                    all the time in the desert, in the ocean, lips
rush lips, you close in on the folds of my
                    body under blankets. The electric bill, food
stamps, a neighborhood clinic days of the week;
                    now you cook cabbage, now we go see Grover
Washington, Jr., now you kiss my wrist halfway into
                    Vincent, Francoise, Paul & the Others. Lost
weight disappears into the atmosphere, I see
                    you come you see me come, dry brown leaves
hang on the loose mosquito screen, trees
                    in the wind sift across the streetlight
out the high windowpane falling asleep.
                    None of this stops. Walnuts, ginseng, hides.
you get angry, keep things inside. You
                    smile, take walks with me. Alone, men whistle
at you from convertibles, you alter your art when
                    it becomes too easy, start sentences with
is so as not to waste time. Or your legs or
                    my heart, two minds ship off the furthest runway
lapping the juices of a mint condition spirit.

FIFTY-SIXTH HYMN

The yellow bird swans through
the operatic air this morning. How welcome
                                I feel in the world!
You rise early and bathe.
There's no doubt we are mediterranean
                                people, meant by all the mama-sans
to kiss and engage
young, more than just looks,
                                let's paint the bathroom white!
Johann Sebastian with the sunday paper,
what could the stars be up to
this time in Parade? Eat
                                grape nuts, how nice at times
to be American. Wars have ended,
I feel like fat Stendhal
wanting to marry in his fifties
                                the landlord's 18 year old daughter.
Into the dog days, one line moves
                                me as you slowly unravel
as you slowly turn
                                as you apply more color to the canvas
as the yellow bird lands on my shoulder
                                as today.

FIFTY-SEVENTH HYMN

The red pickup with white letters
C H E V E R O L E T is parked under one streetlight;
under the light of the other
a small mimosa perfectly still,
crickets & dogs. The garbage
passive on the sidewalk for collection, a black
teenager bops down Humphreys St.
snapping his fingers. Chipped white
clapboard houses in the semi-dark as if
in another universe a full moon
the mottled cat a large Purina grainary.
This is our neighborhood, stop, sirens
in the September night. I read
an AP story about a young woman in New York
arrested when her dog ate her five day old baby;
she had gone out for money to buy food.
the 15 lb. dog, the infant, the brown rug they all
slept on, just a folding wooden chair, welfare.
Busted for negligence. From Ohio, the baby
the result of an unreported rape.
the cactus on our porch needs watering,
this is how much I love you
and this and this.
Distant automobiles travel the city.
You sleep for another night of your life, permanent
green, light on your fingers how
fortunate, I think, autumn, we all are.

FIFTY-FOURTH HYMN

You would like to cultivate lovers
into the slick orb of your fantasy, the way
we all do, hanging on till
the fever matures into a natural
unfantastic ease & passing out,
the lights in the boxcar
dimmed in wait for your very next blossom.
You shuffle through men for the fuck
that will turn into the wild card
your futre can eat and call itself full.
How rich a world you could arrange
with the correct account behind you
admiring your taste and, as in a novel,
you scout forever. I am not unaware
of contradictions as I love you
deeply in full command of my senses.
We may or may not stay together,
We may or may not move to Italy.
What a strange & cunning reversal
of your "my fate is out of my hands"
attitude as I wait here speechless,
a christian without five aces.
The rain moves in & I take my constitutional;
the instances of your happiness
burned into my eyes like pillars of salt.
You know, my darling, I could end
this poem on an ironic note
but I prefer, with forethought, no
end at all. We somehow manage smoothness
most of the time.

FIFTY-FIFTH HYMN

All these things accomplished: how we
found a funky, high-ceilinged house
to radiate from, bought buffalo sandals,
had a swim, how you chop cabbage
to Bill Evans & Tony Bennett. There is
a language I've worn since birth
you charm me your touch
drinks me full up hard by a cafe
most anyone could relate to in a pinch
how we sit here and words are not
yellow jackets or wasps unnecessary
messages at all. What could love be,
this sharing of personal hygiene & space,
your cold, my lust, our two desks
aglow in opposite corners of the room
mute terrific untranslateable evidence.

14, 1975
7 RACE
June 14, 1975
3
4
3

FIFTY-THIRD HYMN

I would like, at times, dressed
as a shiek to be a street punk
with nothing to do but love you
you know, satisfy your every etc.
as no man can lay big bucks
on you, destroy chinchillas, strictly
pre-war chateau wines, that sort
of thing, with feeling, spiritual
communion, the whole batch
like the finest of men to be attentive
& strong, loose, handsome almost
imaginary but not quite
speaking six languages a prince, really
no more food stamp lines or cockroach
pellets instead round-the-world jaunts
you wanna be in a Hollywood movie
snapping fingers & jowls, hocks, knuckles,
ribs on sale constantly BBQ sauce
on the right side of the tracks
no longer this bare existence
from the dangling light bulb we need
color tvs and yachts you are
my harem the lamp I rub
the lamp post I hang out under
while pedestrians run over each other
and the world exhausts itself

POSTWORD

These poems carry within themselves a certain future which has nowhere to go. I am here now but not by the grace of that long-ago future, instead through some miracle of savagery way beyond anything conceivable then. Is it not always so? What interests me is the surface of a world. I live across the street from the top mafioso restaurant in New York and the art teacher next door dies from natural causes in the middle of fashionable conversation. Sleep murders all ambition.

I wanted to be romantic while there was still time. Looking at the fire escape is, almost thirty, never having had to say, "This is it, Buster!" Yet it has all grown quite different. Still American, I am torn between high fashion and chinese politics and to clear my mind, I am seriously considering the donation of my body to the third world. It must be frightening to consider that they might not accept it. These are all things that nip at us day by day, turning our hearts into dreams and our minds into puddings.

In rereading these works of several years back, they seem to me now illuminants of a path already residual, which has value in direct relationship to the distance I have travelled from it. For the average reader I cannot say. Call them early exercises or call them love poems, they are the records of a process which has since gotten so large as to require the mining of prose.

Charlie Walsh
The Cotton Club
3.8.78

My Summer Vacation is published by As Is / So & So Press in an edition of 500 copies, 36 of which are lettered A-Z and numbered 1-10 and signed by the poet.

As Is / So & So Books
John Marron, ed. (joma)
1730 Carleton Street
Berkeley, California 94703

SIXTIETH HYMN

Mere black metal composed
with chrome made overseas
hung from the neck, dead,
of human beings seeing flashes
of topographical brilliance, pretend
sometimes that I am real &/or relaxed
with you as subject. Shape light
amidst your curves & shadows into
my body, bend it, mirror, you become
the reversed frozen image of my innate
function, all I want in the available
illumination, the only plausible focal
point for a perfect exposure. I am
incompetent to bless who made your
eyes, my lens opens, f64, to soak
you up in the background haze.
I watch the clock as you develop,
as you fix, rinse, become full size.
But you still move
me, your colors alter, the background
ticks away, how large
your activity swells on this plane
of mortals, how three dimensional
and warm I feel in your hands.
In the recent cold snap, you forgot me
on idle in the glove compartment,
like white silk saved for full dress occasions.
snapshots of tundra and wasted
watermelon fields shrivelled my electric
eye, exhausted frames hungered for even
a casual you. Now
I am in peak condition, now my warranties
are once more effective, now
my microseconds thrill to your touch.

75
8 RACE June 12, 1975
8 R
MIRROR
IMAGE
7
7
4
4
PHOTO FOR SHOW
BY JONES PRECISION PHOTO FINISH
DOWNS LINCOLN DOWNS LINCOLN DOWNS LINCOLN